Purrs of Wisdom

Enlightenment, Feline Style

By Ingrid King

"Generous, compassionate and insightful, Ingrid King's writing combines practical suggestions with timeless wisdom of value to us all."

– **David Michie**, international bestselling author of
The Dalai Lama's Cat

636.8
KIN

2-21-16 HL

For everyone whose heart has been opened by the love of a cat, and in loving memory of Buckley, the original feline master teacher, and Amber, the original conscious cat.

Also by Ingrid King

Buckley's Story: Lessons from a Feline Master Teacher

Tortitude: The BIG Book of Cats with a BIG Attitude

Adventures in Veterinary Medicine: What Working in Veterinary Hospitals Taught Me About Life, Love and Myself

Praise for **Purrs of Wisdom: Conscious Living, Feline Style**

"**Purrs of Wisdom,** by Ingrid King, is a treat for anyone who is enchanted by all things feline! The book is an exploration of lessons on living a joyful and inspired life, learned from the many magical cats who have shared the author's journey.

I found gifts on every page, but the section titled Lessons from a Maple Tree especially touched my heart. The author talks about taking time out of her busy day to soak up the tree's magnificent colors when the leaves change in the fall. 'Doing nothing without feeling guilty' is a lesson she learned from her cats. Ingrid's words were a gentle reminder to this fast-paced former New Yorker to look to my own kitties for guidance when my world seems to be spinning a bit too quickly.

Purrs of Wisdom is sure to be a treasured addition to any cat lover's library!"

– **Christine Davis,** Author of **For Every Cat An Angel and Forever Paws**

"Reading this collection of feline-inspired essays and life lessons gave me several 'AHA!' moments. Purrs of Wisdom is a refreshing read that packs a deceptively powerful punch and provides helpful recipes for finding your bliss. Ingrid King writes with compassion for those who struggle along as 'life happens.' The gifted writer offers nearly poetic insight on how to manage the angst, as well as to recognize the "why" behind such things. You'll want to savor each individual chapter and purr-haps bookmark and revisit those that strike a personal chord. And of course, read aloud to your favorite feline companion!"

– **Amy Shojai**, bestselling author of more than two dozen pet books

"**Purrs of Wisdom** is the perfect book for anyone who loves cats – and has an interest in living life to the fullest, with a positive and peaceful outlook – just like a cat does! It spoke to me on several levels and is sure to become a well-thumbed volume as I continue on my life's journey."

– **Ann Brightman**, Managing Editor, **Animal Wellness Magazine**

"In this guide to living spiritually and creatively in a world that isn't always quite comfortable with either quality, King, a keenly intuitive writer, draws upon the lessons she has learned from her beloved feline friends, weaving them deftly together with her own experiences."

– **T.J. Banks**, Author of **Sketch People: Stories Along the Way and Catsong**

Praise for **Buckley's Story: Lessons from a Feline Master Teacher**

"**Buckley's Story** is a true celebration of the bond between pets and their humans. This story of a 'gimpy' little tortoiseshell cat with a huge heart who changed her human's life in unexpected ways shows us how pets teach us universal lessons about living a joyful life, how caring for a terminally ill pet can deepen this special bond, and how to navigate the devastating grief that comes with losing a beloved animal companion."

– **Dr. Marty Becker**, "America's Veterinarian" and author of **The Healing Power of Pets: Harnessing the Amazing Ability of Pets To Make and Keep People Happy and Healthy**

"Ingrid King loves animals, and in **Buckley's Story** she leads us through how these precious creatures — in particular, one 'gimpy tortie' named Buckley — can teach us how to open our hearts to the world."

– **Clea Simon**, author of **The Feline Mystique: On the Mysterious Connection Between Women and Cats**

"For those of us who think–or, rather, know–that cats have a thing or two to teach us in this life, you'll appreciate Ingrid King's story about her cat Buckley."

– **Megan McMorris**, Editor of **Cat Women – Female Writers on their Feline Friends**

Praise for **Adventures in Veterinary Medicine**

"In reading Ingrid King's **Adventures in Veterinary Medicine**, I was taken back to the feeling of excitement experienced when I first worked as a technician during my college years. From learning the initial approach to a fractious cat to the inevitable frustrations associated with being part of a professional care giving team, I've been there too. It's refreshing to feel such resonance with an author who has dedicated herself to the betterment of animal health and welfare in veterinary practice and in her media career."

   – **Patrick Mahaney,** VMD, owner and president of California Pet Acupuncture and Wellness and writer/blogger

"As a 'veteran veterinarian' with more than 30 years in practice, I found myself nodding in recognition throughout Ingrid King's heartwarming book. Take a look behind the scenes at my beloved profession, and the people and pets who make veterinary medicine a rewarding adventure. You won't regret it, I promise."

   – **Dr. Marty Becker,** "America's Veterinarian" and resident veterinarian for **The Dr. Oz Show**

"I loved **Adventures in Veterinary Medicine**. Ingrid King's stories are both poignant and entertaining. Her narrative very accurately reveals what life is like for those of us in the veterinary profession. A quick, easy read, I highly recommend this book."

   – **Lorie Huston,** DVM, veterinarian and award winning writer/blogger

More Praise for Ingrid King's Writing

"Ingrid King defines what it is to be a "cat person." She doesn't just live with them, observe and write about them; rather, she delves deeper, reflecting a natural sense of empathy and kinship with cats. There is an intrinsic bond with the feline world on display in casual conversation with Ingrid, as well as in her writing. Ingrid brings us closer to understanding the everyday reality of cats and, finally, what we can learn about our own lives through better appreciating theirs."

–**Jackson Galaxy,** Host of Animal Planet's **My Cat From Hell**

Table of Contents

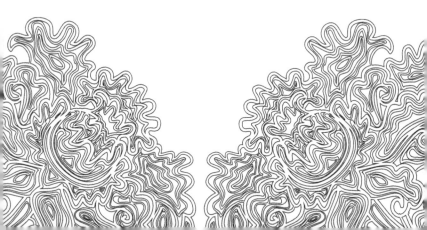

Introduction

For the past five years, I've been writing a column titled "Conscious Cat Sunday." These essays are a bit of a departure from our usual fare on The Conscious Cat, which focuses on cat health, nutrition, behavior and lifestyle. The Sunday columns feature lessons in conscious living, inspired by the cats who have shared my life. They have become wildly popular; perhaps this is because they are not really that much different from our regular focus after all. Conscious Cat readers want their cats to be happy, and since cats are sensitive creatures who pick up on their human's emotions, there is a direct correlation between the human's happiness and the cat's. It therefore makes sense that these practical, spiritual, transformational and philosophical purrs of wisdom appeal to readers who are in search of a better life, for themselves and their cats.

I have always believed that animals come into our lives to teach us. First and foremost, they teach us about unconditional love. But they also teach us to stretch and grow, to reach beyond our self-imposed limits, and to expand our consciousness. Even though I didn't have cats until I was in my early 20's, the cats I have shared my life with since have all turned out to be amazing teachers.

I was not allowed to have pets as a child. The apartment building I grew up in would not permit them, but I would temporarily adopt cats for the duration of almost every family vacation. I grew up in Germany, and in those days, a typical vacation meant that you went to one place and stayed there for two or three weeks at a time. We stayed at small bed-and-breakfasts or rented a vacation condo, and somehow, at every place we stayed, we would either find a resident cat or two, or there would be a number of stray cats hanging around the property. The times I spent with these cats make up some of my happiest childhood memories.

I got my first cat when I was in my twenties. Feebee was a grey tabby cat who was born in the Shenandoah Valley of Virginia to a cat named Blue, who belonged to a childhood friend of my former husband. For fifteen and a half years, Feebee was the love of my life. He saw me through my divorce as well as the death of my mother. He was my primary emotional support during those dark days. If it wasn't for him, you might not be reading this book.

He was also instrumental in guiding me toward a new career. I was increasingly unhappy with my corporate job but had no clear sense of what I was meant to be doing with my life. Then Feebee took matters into his own paws, so to speak, and developed bladder stones. The time we spent at veterinary hospitals for diagnosis, treatment, and surgery led me to change careers. I started volunteering and then working part time at veterinary hospitals, which eventually led to a full-time position managing an animal hospital—a position that came with an office cat with a very distinct personality. Virginia, a beautiful tortoiseshell cat, loved me fiercely, and made my dream of a fulfilling career complete. Whenever I had visualized my perfect job, that dream had always included a cat sleeping in a sunny spot on my desk. One of Virginia's favorite sleeping places was the spot right next to my computer, in front of a sunny window.

Working at various animal hospitals led to many encounters with a large variety of special cats and dogs. I share some of the lessons learned from those encounters in **Adventures in Veterinary Medicine: What Working in Veterinary Hospitals Taught Me About Life, Love and Myself.**

Several years later, Feebee lost his battle with lymphoma. Three months after he passed away, Amber came into my life. She was a stray who was brought to the animal hospital with her five kittens. She was emaciated and scrawny, but even then, her eventual beauty was evident. She was a dark tortoiseshell color, with an amber-colored, heart-shaped spot on top of her head, which inspired her name. Her kittens were adopted out to new homes in fairly rapid succession, but nobody was interested in the beautiful mommy cat. I did not think I was ready for another cat; the wound from Feebee's passing was still very fresh and raw. But coming home to an empty house was becoming increasingly difficult, so one day I decided to take Amber home "just for the weekend." She never returned to the animal hospital. Her gentle, loving, wise presence—not to mention her almost constant purr—brought love and affection into my life every day for ten years. She was also the inspiration for The Conscious Cat.

Next came Buckley. Even though she was only in my life for three short years, this joyful, enthusiastic, and affectionate tortoiseshell cat changed my life in ways I never could have imagined. My journey with Buckley from the time that she became my office cat at the animal hospital to joining Amber and me at home, helping her manage her heart disease, and ultimately assisting her through the final transition, is covered in **Buckley's Story: Lessons from a Feline Master Teacher.**

I now share my life with Allegra and Ruby, two young tortoiseshell cats who are carrying on the tradition of teaching cats in my life. I adopted them both as kittens, Allegra in 2010, and Ruby in 2011. At five (Ruby) and six (Allegra) years old, they've already shown me that they're continuing the tradition of feline master teachers in my life.

I hope this collection of essays will inspire you, remind you of lessons your own cats may have taught you, provide "aha" moments, or simply make you smile.

These essays are best enjoyed with a cat curled up on your lap.

Practical Purrs

The Benefits of Stretching

Allegra
Photo by: Ingrid King

Expand your experiences regularly so every stretch
won't feel like your first.
– Gina Greenlee

Stretching is an important part of healthy living: benefits range from increased flexibility and mobility to better athletic performance and decreased risk of injury. A regular stretching program has been part of my daily routine for more than 30 years. I've had minor back problems ever since I was a young adult, and twice daily stretching exercises have most likely helped save my back again and again.

And who better to teach us the importance of stretching than our cats? Have you ever seen a cat get up from a nap without thoroughly stretching first?

Stretching is actually an instinctive activity: most people stretch without having to be reminded before they get out of bed. It appears that our bodies naturally protect us from injuring ourselves by moving too fast after a period of inactivity. Depending on your age, and what kind of physical condition you're in, you may find that even getting up from being seated at your desk for a long period of time will result in aches and pains unless you stretch first.

There are multiple benefits to stretching:

- Improved circulation. The increased blood flow to the muscles removes toxins, and can help speed up recovery from injuries.

- Better posture, balance and coordination. Stretching prevents muscles from tightening up, and the increase in flexibility provides better balance.

- Stress relief. Tight muscles, especially in the neck and shoulders, are often a by-product of stress.

- **Increased flexibility.** Do you remember a time when you could touch your big toe to your nose? For most of us, those days are long gone. While stretching may not restore the level of flexibility we had as a child, it can go a long way toward making ordinary tasks such as bending down to tie your shoes easier.

- **Ease lower back pain.** Tight muscles in the lower back, hamstrings, buttocks and hips are the most common causes of lower back pain. I can attest to the fact that a regular stretching routine is key to maintaining good back health.

Let your cats remind you to make stretching a regular part of your daily routine. Your body will thank you for it.

Declutter Your Life

Amber
Photo by: Ingrid King

Life is really simple, but we insist on
making it complicated.
- Confucius

The physical surroundings we live in every day in our homes, offices and cars have a strong impact on us. Cluttered environments drain your energy. Just think about the last time you organized a drawer or cleaned your car. Do you remember how accomplished you felt, and how you were able to approach the rest of your day from a much lighter perspective? That's because you released stagnant, cluttered energy.

Allegra, Ruby, and I periodically work on decluttering together. Since I frequently receive cat toys, scratchers, beds and other cat products, our home can easily look like the inside of a pet store, so periodically we go through everything and decide what to keep and what to donate to local rescue groups.

I'm pretty organized in general. I don't function well with visible disorder, but when deadlines loom and I'm working on multiple projects, my desk tends to get a bit more cluttered than I like. When I start feeling stressed just by looking at my desk, I know it's time to start organizing papers into folders and putting things away. I'm not nearly as good about the space inside my desk drawers or closet, but I usually reach a point where I simply can't stand it anymore, and I take an hour or two to set things right.

I always feel lighter after getting rid of clutter and things that no longer serve me, and I highly recommend the practice.

With a little feline assistance, decluttering doesn't have to be a chore. Make a game of it with your cats: as you get rid of papers, toss some balled up paper for your cats to chase. Bringing out boxes to collect items you're going to get rid of is sure to be a hit with most cats (just make sure to check for any cats inside before tossing!).

7 Habits of Happy Cats and Humans

Peekaboo, Ft. Lauderdale, FL

Photo by: Jodi Ziskin

Motivation is what gets you started. Habit is
what keeps you going.
- Jim Ryun

Contrary to what many people believe, happiness is a choice. Happy people are happy because they make themselves happy. They maintain a mostly positive outlook, and practice habits that make their lives happier. Not surprisingly, our cats already practice many of these habits.

1. Live in the present. Cats live in the moment. When they're lazing about in a sun puddle, they don't worry about when the next sun puddle will show up – they simply enjoy the pleasure of the warmth on their fur, right now, in this present moment.

2. Wake up at the same time every morning. Have you ever noticed how many successful and happy people are early risers? Waking up at the same time each day keeps your circadian rhythm in balance, which keeps you calmer and more centered and also increases productivity.

3. Eat well. Junk food may make you feel good for a brief period of time, but in the long run, it will make you feel sluggish, not to mention take a toll on your health. Everything you eat affects not just your physical, but also your emotional and mental health. Eating fresh, whole, minimally processed foods will keep human and feline bodies and minds in good shape.

4. Exercise. Regular exercise is one of the best ways I know of to stay happy and healthy, and this goes for humans and cats.

5. Meditate. Even a five-minute mini-meditation at the beginning of your day can set the tone for a less stressful day. Better yet, take a few mini-meditation breaks during the day.

6. Practice gratitude. Gratitude makes you happy. Research by Dr. Robert Emmons of the University of California at Davis into the psychology of gratitude has shown that people who practice gratitude are 25% happier. They are more optimistic about the future and feel better about their lives.

7. Accept what is. One of the greatest sources of unhappiness is the inability to accept things as they are. Accepting what is, without wishing things were different, is the key to living a positive, present life.

Why Conscious Living is Good for Your Cats

Angel, Magnolia, TX

Photo by: Bari Dubois

Happiness is a conscious choice, not an automatic response.
- Mildred Barthel

The tag line of The Conscious Cat is "Conscious Living, Health and Happiness for Cats and their Humans." I choose this motto, along with the name for the site, because I believe that living consciously is the key to happiness for all of us.

What is conscious living? The definition of the word conscious is "to be aware of one's own existence, sensations, thoughts and surroundings." It also means "being fully aware or sensitive to something," "aware of oneself," and "deliberate and intentional." All these terms take us right to the heart of what conscious living means.

Conscious living means making choices that are in alignment with who we really are at our core. We make choices about everything we do all day long, from the food we eat and feed our cats, to the products we use on ourselves and in our environment. The more we make these conscious choices, the more whole our lives will become, and the happier we will be – and so will our cats.

There are three components of conscious living: health and nutrition, environment, and mental, emotional and spiritual health. We have to tend to all three of them, for ourselves and for our cats, to ensure that we live a balanced and happy life.

Health and Nutrition. Nutrition is the foundation of good health for both ourselves and our cats. We can't change genetics, but we can control what we put into our bodies, and what we feed our cats. You'll find lots of information on species appropriate feline nutrition as well as a wealth of feline health topics on The Conscious Cat.

Environment. There are two parts to the component of environment: the space we live in, and the products we use in that space. At their core, cats are still wild animals, and while we've invited them into our homes to share our lives, we can't expect them to completely give up all their instincts. We have to look at our living space from the cat's point of view and provide an environment that keeps them stimulated.

Make your home cat friendly by creating a kitty paradise of cat trees, shelves, scratching posts, cat cubes and tunnels. By providing plenty of options, you'll avoid behavior issues and keep your cats happy.

Don't use commercial cleaning products that contain harmful chemicals. Many of these products can be extremely toxic, and even deadly. Cats are especially susceptible since they groom themselves by licking and as a result ingest anything that comes in contact with their feet or fur. Use cat-friendly cleaning products instead – they're better for your cats, for you, and the planet.

Mental, emotional and spiritual health. Cats are good for our health. Studies have shown that simply petting a cat (or dog, for that matter) lowers our blood pressure. A 10-year study at the University of Minnesota Stroke Center found that cat owners were 40% less likely to have a heart attack than non-cat owners.

Cats are not just good for our physical health, they're good for our mental, emotional and spiritual health. Cats teach us to live in the moment, to slow down, and to not take life quite so seriously. And they open our hearts; sometimes, in a very big way.

The argument for conscious living is compelling. And it's not just good for us, it's good for our cats.

Why Cats Don't Make New Year's Resolutions

Allegra
Photo by: Ingrid King

May all your troubles last as long as your
New Year's resolutions.
– Joey Adams

When I asked Allegra and Ruby about their New Year's resolutions, they gave me a funny look. Allegra said New Year's resolutions are a silly human invention. She said cats live in the moment and don't worry about what they should be doing next, so they don't need resolutions. Ruby said she resolves to get more treats this year.

I stopped making New Year's resolutions several years ago. Since I still like the idea of the "fresh start" a new year offers, I set New Year's intentions instead. I think New Year's resolutions are destined to fail, because there's an inherent flaw in the term "resolution." According to Merriam Webster, the definition of resolution is "the act of determining." There's nothing there that says we're actually going to do something. This is why I prefer to set New Year's intentions. The definition of intention is "a determination to act in a certain way." The difference is subtle, but one (intention) implies that we are actually determined to do something differently, whereas the other (resolution) simply states that we've decided to change something.

Setting an intention is nothing more than focusing your thoughts on what you would like to create in your life. That doesn't mean you won't still have to do the work, but it sets you up for a more successful outcome.

Make setting intentions a daily practice, rather than a once a year exercise. At the beginning of each day, spend some time meditating and clearing your head, and set the intention for that day. This is not so much a to-do list as it is setting the tone for the day ahead. Rather than focusing on getting x, y and z done, focus on how you want to accomplish the day's tasks, and on making sure that there is balance in your day. For me, that includes making time for reading, time with friends (some days this may only happen online, other days, it will happen in "real life") and of course, time for Allegra and Ruby, in addition to work. At the end of each day, evaluate whether you've followed your intentions, or whether things need to be tweaked for the next day.

Allegra and Ruby think this is much ado about nothing. Allegra says if humans would just focus on living in the moment, all the rest will fall into place. Ruby says she'll intend to get more treats every day.

![Cat on keyboard]

Taming Technology

Abby, Decatur, AL
Photo by: Toni Nicholson

Technology makes it possible for people to gain
control over everything, except over technology.
– John Tudor

I spend much of my day online, whether it's doing research for an article, interacting with friends and fans on our various social media sites, or responding to the never-ending flow of email. I also have an iPhone and iPad to keep me connected to The Conscious Cat site, social media and email when I'm not at my computer. And I know I'm not alone. Technology has become a part of our everyday lives, for better or for worse.

I love technology, but... I love the world of email, blogs, social media and other forms of online communication and the opportunities it presents. I especially love how it has changed how we meet people and form friendships in ways we never could have imagined even ten years ago. Technology has allowed me to make contact with people I never could have met in real life. Whether it's the author I've admired for decades, or the veterinarian whose articles I've only read in journals before, or the many fellow cat people who share my love for these incredibly fascinating and wonderful creatures – I treasure all of these relationships. Some of them have turned into real-life friendships.

But all this connection comes with challenges. This massive influx of messages, notifications, and never-ending flow of information can crush your spirit if you let it. It can take over your world, and not in a good way. Coping with this much information can easily become overwhelming, and it's insidious, because you may not even notice how it can increase your stress levels, one email and one notification at a time.

The seduction of technology. I can't imagine a life without technology, nor would I want to. But I, like so many others, need to find better ways to manage the role technology plays in my life. There is a seductive quality to all this connectedness. It feels good to have others validate what you share, even if it's only with the click of a "like" button.

There's actually science behind that good feeling that you get from that "like": it creates compulsive behavior by tapping into the brain's reward circuit and operant conditioning: the association of stimulus and reward. Every time you get that "like," you get a little dopamine hit. Dopamine is one of the neurotransmitters that make you feel good. Receiving that email, text, or Facebook comment sends a message to your brain that says "Yay! Somebody loves me!" In time, your brain comes to associate this feeling with the notification alert sound on your device, and releases a squirt of dopamine each time it hears the signal.

As if this weren't bad enough, after you check that e-mail or that Facebook comment, your dopamine levels dip below normal, so you need another hit just to get your levels back to normal. If you've ever sat at your computer and hit the "get new mail" button over and over and wondered why on earth you're doing that, now you know.

I find all of this a bit scary, and I've been spending quite a bit of time lately thinking about how to manage the role technology plays in my life better. I find it very difficult to unplug completely. As a self-employed freelance writer and blogger, being online can easily become a 24/7 proposition. But I'm also finding that I can't let it take over my life. I started to think about what I can do to tame the technology beast in my life. Here's what I came up with:

Setting boundaries. I don't check email as soon as I get up. I feed Allegra and Ruby first! I set a time limit for myself for the amount of time I spend on social media sites. I shut down my computer after dinner. I tried unplugging completely, but found myself checking email on either my phone or iPad a few more times throughout the evening, and then I'd beat myself up over doing that. So now I'm "allowed" to check email up until 7pm, but that's absolutely my cut off. Interestingly, I found that on nights when I violate my self-imposed curfew and use the iPad too close to bedtime, I don't sleep well.

Unplug for short periods of time. While I would love to be able to unplug for an entire day, I just haven't been able to do it. I'm working up to it, though. In the meantime, I don't take my phone with me on my daily walks. That one hour each day is sacred. No phone, just me, my thoughts, and the nature around me.

Don't let technology interfere with "real" face to face contact. There's nothing more irritating to me than having lunch with someone who keeps a constant eye on their smartphone.

No one is going to die if you unplug. Let's face it: unless you're a physician or a veterinarian on call, you do not need to be available 24/7. No one is going to die if you don't respond to an email, text or message until your regular business hours.

In a lot of ways, taming technology is like taming a feral cat – it takes a great deal of commitment, dedication, and patience.

Support Charities that Don't Test on Animals

Kayla, Ft. Lauderdale, FL

Photo by: Jodi Ziskin

The greatness of a nation and its moral progress can
be judged by how its animals are treated.
– **Mahatma Gandhi**

It's difficult to say no to all the requests that all of us see almost every day to donate to charities that are seeking a cure for a disease. Often, these requests come from friends who are supporting the charity through walks, bike races, and other activities. And how many of us really take the time to find out how our donation will be used? We want to think that our money goes toward reducing suffering, but if the charity supports animal testing, that may not be the case.

Animal experiments are cruel and unnecessary. There are plenty of arguments that animal testing is a necessary part of medical research, and that finding a cure for human diseases outweighs the suffering this research causes to innocent animals. However, scientists are increasingly seeing that the results of animal experiments are not directly applicable to humans. Doctors Against Animal Experiments, a German organization advocating animal-free research, quotes a study conducted by the pharmaceutical company Pfizer. The study came to the conclusion that "one would be better off tossing a coin than relying on animal experiments to answer the question of carcinogenic substances. Only 5 – 25% of the substances harmful to humans also have adverse effects on the experimental animals. Tossing a coin delivers better results."

Does your favorite charity support animal testing? I've gotten into the habit of checking whether a charity supports animal testing before making any type of donation. The Physicians' Committee for Responsible Medicine maintains an extensive searchable database via its Humane Charity Seal program. For more information, and to search the charity database, visit HumaneSeal.org.

How Choosing the Right
Cosmetics Benefits Your Cats

Allegra and Ruby

Photo by: Ingrid King

A life lived of choice is a life of conscious action.
– Neale Donald Walsh

Conscious living means making conscious choices about all aspects of our lives, including the cosmetics we use on ourselves. Using chemical-free cosmetics is not just better for you, it's also better for your cats, because not only does your skin come in contact with those products, but so do your cat's fur, paws, and mouth – and some of the chemicals used in conventional cosmetics can be harmful to both humans and cats.

Harmful chemicals in cosmetics. The skin is our largest organ, and it easily absorbs what is put on it. This means that it not only absorbs the beneficial ingredients in cosmetics, but also the chemicals, especially with repeat exposure. One third of the cosmetics products currently on the market contain chemicals that are linked to cancer. Of the more than 10,000 ingredients used in personal care products, close to 90% have not undergone any safety testing. Given those statistics, doesn't it make sense to be conscious about the products you use on your skin every day?

The European Union Cosmetics Directive, established in 1976 and revised and updated multiple times since, bans the use of chemicals that are known or strongly suspected to cause cancer, mutations and birth defects. In 2004, the directive was amended to require all companies selling cosmetics in the EU to remove these chemicals from their products. Many US companies sell their products on the European market and have been required to reformulate their products. However, just because a company sells its products in Europe does not mean that the same products you purchase here in the US meet EU standards.

Read labels carefully. Read your labels before purchasing cosmetics. Just because something is labeled "natural" and has pretty designs of wholesome ingredients on the label does not necessarily mean that it is chemical-free. Look for brands that comply with EU regulations.

Cruelty-free products. Another consideration that is important when choosing cosmetics and personal care products is that they are not tested on animals. Look for the Leaping Bunny logo – it provides the best assurance that the products you use are cruelty-free and have not been tested on animals. Incidentally, in 2013, the European Union banned the import and sale of cosmetics containing ingredients tested on animals.

I switched to mostly chemical-free cosmetics years ago, and it's a good thing I did: one of Allegra's favorite things to do is to lick my hands after I put on hand lotion. And while I don't let her do it for very long, because I don't think that too much of even the most "natural" hand lotion is good for her, at least I don't have to worry about her ingesting harmful chemicals while I let her have a little fun.

It's probably next to impossible to avoid all chemicals in the products we use in our homes and around our cats, but an informed and conscious choice goes a long way toward healthier cats and healthier humans.

Weather Anxiety

Allegra
Photo by: Ingrid King

It is best to read the weather forecast before
praying for rain.
– Mark Twain

It seems that we never just have weather anymore. Every day, we see warnings about severe storms, floods, blizzards and other weather hazards that used to be the exception, not the new normal. It's hard not to feel anxious when you're bombarded with advisories and dire warnings everywhere you look. All of this has created something that is increasingly being looked at a psychological disorder: weather anxiety. Our obsession with the weather, fed by the media, seems to be out of control. The Huffington Post reports that checking weather apps is the number one smartphone use.

Obviously, concern about approaching severe weather is normal, and it's important to stay informed, but if your thoughts spiral out of control into worst case scenarios and prevent you from functioning normally, you may suffer from weather anxiety.

Cats pick up on human weather anxiety. Severe weather can also be stressful for our cats. Howling winds, heavy rain and thunderstorms can be very frightening even for indoor cats. Behaviorists are not sure which part of the storm frightens pets the most – the lightning flashes and thunder, the winds blowing around the house or the sound of rain hitting the roof. Some pets even show signs of anxiety an hour or more before a storm hits, leading to the theory that they are reacting to changes in barometric pressure.
If you suffer from weather anxiety, chances are that your cats will pick up on your energy and be more afraid as well, so finding ways to deal with your anxiety will not only help you, it will also keep your cats calmer.

Get control of your weather anxiety. If you find yourself getting anxious when the forecast calls for severe weather, try one or more of the following:

- Limit watching the weather forecast, and find a source that presents the information without the hype. This can be challenging in this current media climate, but there are outlets that limit sensationalism and stick to mostly facts.

- Make reasonable preparations. Having a plan will make you feel more in control.

- Stay informed about weather conditions, but don't become obsessed with up to the minute predictions.

- Stay in touch with friends and loved ones, especially if you live alone.

I'll admit to getting a little anxious before and during severe weather. Allegra, who is the more sensitive of my two girls, always picks up on my anxiety, which actually helps me because it forces me to remember to stay calm.

Spiritual Purrs

The Culture of Fear

Obi, Ft. Lauderdale, FL

Photo by: Jodi Ziskin

Let go of fear, embrace change, and move toward joy.
– Buckley

Fear is a normal response to a threatening stimulus or situation. Without the fear response, neither cats nor humans would survive. Fear prepares us for fight or flight. While our domesticated cats may not have to worry about survival and may not encounter anything more frightening than the vacuum cleaner or a thunderstorm, some fears may be hardwired. The good news is that, with proper support from their guardians, cats can get over their fears. Allegra used to be terrified of bad weather, but has come a long way in the past year in overcoming her fears.

But what happens when fear becomes a part of our daily lives?

We live in a culture of fear. There has never been a time when people have been afraid of so much. Three out of four Americans say they feel more fearful today than they did twenty years ago. The media would have us believe that we need to be afraid of everything: the weather, the economy, terrorism, the government, threats to our health. If you listen to them, Armageddon is just around the corner. We get warnings via e-mail, text and social media. Our online lives are driven by fear of security breaches with the passwords, codes and questions required to access the sites we visit (how many of us really remember the kid's name three doors down from us on the first street we ever lived on?).

Nature did not design the fear response to be a non-stop occurrence. When it kicks in, higher levels of adrenalin and cortisol are released into our system. This leads to an increase in blood pressure and heart rate and delivers increased oxygen and energy to muscles. While this is necessary in a real fear situation, it is ultimately a stress response, and we know that prolonged periods of stress lead to illness – in ourselves, and in our cats.

It's hard not to buy into this culture of fear, but there are ways to cope:

Don't watch the news. This is the single most effective step I know of toward better mental, emotional, spiritual and physical health. You are discerning about what you put into your body – why not use that same judgment about what you allow to enter into your mind? If you must watch the news, don't watch first thing in the morning or just before you go to bed.

Change the story in your mind. Before you buy into one of those fear-based stories, use common sense. How likely is it that this thing you fear will happen? You have the power to control your thoughts: change your story to something rational.

Set boundaries. Turn off some of the alerts you get. Do you really need daily stock market updates? Do you need an email each time a weather alert is issued?

Meditate. Meditation, or any other form of structured spiritual practice, will help you shift your mindset from one of fear to one of love and connectedness with something greater than you.

Pet your cats. Studies have shown that petting a cat can lower your blood pressure and reduce your heart rate. It's impossible to be fearful when you watch a sleeping cat.

Don't buy into our culture of fear. Create a world where you're in charge of how you feel. If you won't do it for yourself, do it for your cats. Cats are sensitive creatures who pick up on their humans' emotions. If you live in a constant state of fear and stress, so will your cats.

How to Be Content

Pepper, Sydney, Australia

Photo by: Murray Cooper

Be content with what you have; rejoice in the way
things are. When you realize there is nothing lacking,
the whole world belongs to you.

– Lao Tzu

When I think about what contentment looks like, I think of a purring cat. If there's anything that illustrates happiness better, I don't know what that would be. And it doesn't take much for cats to be content: a sunny spot on the floor, a full tummy, a lap to curl up on – those are the ingredients for contentment when you're a cat.

Why is it so hard for humans to reach that same state of contentment? Why do so many of us always look for the next best thing? For some people, the mindset for happiness is a never-ending cycle of always wanting more. Perhaps we'd do well to learn from our cats when it comes to mastering contentment.

Achieving a state of contentment is a mindset change and has nothing to do with making external changes to your life. Try the following:

- **Practice gratitude.** The energy of gratitude is a powerful force. It can shift your mood and your thoughts from a place of scarcity to a place of abundance and joy. Gratitude is about being in the present moment, and appreciating what's around you.

- **Meditate.** Meditation helps you to slow your thoughts, and to connect with your spirit. Taking time to meditate, or simply sit and be still, allows contentment to come to you. Better yet, meditate with your cat.

- **Get out of your head and into your heart.** By opening your heart and connecting with what really matters, you'll view the world differently. One of the best ways I know of opening your heart is by allowing the love of a cat to transform you.

- **Don't compare yourself to others.** Focus on what is unique about you instead, and appreciate your special gifts and talents.

- **Find joy in the simple things.** A perfectly brewed cup of tea or coffee, a book I've been wanting to read, and a cat or two curled up next to me or in my lap: what more does anyone need to be content?

The Value of Doing Nothing

Pearl, Middleburg, VA

Photo by: Nancy McMahon

How beautiful it is to do nothing, and
then rest afterwards.
– Spanish Proverb

We live in such crazy busy times that stress has become the norm for most people, and because of that, most of us don't even realize how stressed we are until we allow ourselves to slow down. It's well known that the more stressed we are, the more damage we do not just to our mental health, but also to our bodies. Our bodies are not designed to distinguish between a real threat – "I'm being chased by a tiger!" – and a looming deadline. Your adrenal glands release the stress hormone cortisol regardless of the trigger, and higher and prolonged cortisol levels in your bloodstream wreak havoc on your system.

This busy lifestyle carries over into what is supposed to be our leisure time. Weekends are filled with activities and errands and social engagements. All of this busyness leaves no time for what is one of the best things you can do for yourself: spend some time doing absolutely nothing.

Doing nothing without feeling guilty is something all my cats have taught me over the years. As a culture, we tend to always feel rushed, and many consider being busy a badge of honor. However, there is great value in doing nothing, in simply being.

We need down time. We need time to relax. If you can't remember the last time you did absolutely nothing, start today. Just sit on the sofa, preferably with a cat or two or three, and just be. Don't think, don't plan. Just sit and read a book, or watch mindless TV, or admire the way your cat's fur looks.

Make doing nothing a daily practice, even if it's only for a few minutes. You'll find that not only will you feel less stressed, you'll actually accomplish more in the long run.

Be Kind to Yourself

Celica Blue, Branford, CT

Photo by: Sally Bahner

Be kind whenever possible. It is always possible.
– The Dalai Lama

Kindness is defined as "the quality of being friendly, generous and compassionate." It's a quality that I look for in almost every person I form any kind of relationship with – it matters that much to me. Kindness to cats, and all animals, is the most important to me, but kindness to other human beings is a close second. One of my pet peeves: people who are unkind to waiters or other service personnel.

Research suggests that positive emotions help contribute to better physical and emotional health. And kindness shouldn't just extend to others, it should also be directed at yourself. While common wisdom may suggest that being kind to yourself is selfish and weak, the opposite is true. When you are kind to yourself, you are taking better care of yourself. And if you don't take care of yourself, you have nothing left to give to others.

Here are some ways to be kind to yourself:

Take care of the basics. Eating whole and nutritious foods, drinking enough water, exercising, and getting enough sleep are all ways of being kind to yourself that will have a positive impact on everything else in your life.

Monitor your thought patterns. Albert Einstein once said that "the most important decision we make is whether we believe we live in a friendly or hostile universe." If you constantly expect the worst to happen and focus on negative thoughts, you will get stuck in a pattern of negative actions and emotions. Reframe your thoughts and retrain your brain. Thinking it won't make it so, but it will put you in a better frame of mind and motivate you to make positive changes.

Lower your expectations. This one is for the perfectionists out there, and I'm including myself in that category. I'm not saying that you should settle for less, but unrealistic expectations, especially when you're dealing with emotionally charged or stressful situations, can make you feel completely out of control. Rather than expecting every day to be the best and happiest day of your life, lowering the bar just a little will allow you to enjoy each small moment.

Focus on solutions. If you've had a rough day, or you're facing a challenging problem, try to focus on solutions rather than on rehashing the issue. Don't beat yourself up over a mistake you may have made – this only erodes your self-esteem. Searching for solutions allows you to take your power back.

Give yourself the gift of time. Spend some time every day doing something that will uplift you. Whether it's 10 minutes of meditation, a half hour walk in the park, or an hour of reading a book, all of these will make a big difference in how you feel about your day. Of course, the easiest and quickest way to uplift you is to spend time with your cats!

Cats are naturally gifted at being kind to themselves. From finding the purrfect sun puddle to asking for affection when they want it, they know how to take care of their needs without apology. Perhaps we'd be wise to look to them for some guidance.

Just Say No to Drama

Conchita, Temple, GA

Photo by: Nikki Mantel

When you are not honoring the present moment by
allowing it to be, you are creating drama.
– Eckhart Tolle

I like a good drama as much as the next person. Intrigue, passion, mystery – what's not to like? But when I say I like drama, I'm talking about fiction, not real life. When it comes to real life drama, I don't want any part of it.

Drama is toxic. Even if you're not a drama queen, you'll still be affected by drama around you. Maybe you have a friend who always seems to be in one crisis or another. Maybe you're the person everyone comes to with their problems. Or maybe you have a tendency to turn small problems into much larger ones.

Drama can be anything from gossiping to constant complaining to being unkind to another person. Drama feels heavy, suffocating and constricting. And it's highly seductive, because once you engage, it becomes difficult to escape.

Regardless of what the level of drama in your life is, I guarantee you that any amount of drama is damaging to your soul. Unfortunately, not getting caught up in drama, even someone else's, is harder than it seems.

Why is it so challenging to disengage from drama? It's because drama queens are energy vampires. They're the complainers, passive-aggressives, and doomsday predicters in your life. Like vampires, they feed off the life force of others around them, and they would love nothing better than to turn you into one of them. Misery loves company. And once you engage with one, their icky energy will contaminate your own energy field, unless you're very careful about protecting yourself.

If there's drama in your life, you need to take a good look at yourself – because chances are, on some level, you're creating it. Are you looking for some excitement in your life? Did you grow up with lots of drama, so being around it feels comfortable? You may be surprised at the answers to these questions.

Make a conscious choice to disengage from the drama in your life. Don't participate in gossip. Don't feed into other peoples' drama. Reconsider unhealthy relationships and get rid of the energy vampires in your life, or limit contact with them as much as possible. If there are people in your life who thrive on drama, let them know you've made a decision to not participate any longer, and invite them to do the same. Communicate honestly and directly with others.

Cats don't like drama, either. They prefer life to be peaceful. They're sensitive to the energy around them, and they tend to take on their human's problems, sometimes, in an effort to heal them. That's not only an awful lot of hard work for a cat, it's also detrimental to their well-being.

You may never be able to completely eliminate drama from your life, but you can choose to not play the game. I guarantee you that your life will be more peaceful. And so will your cats' lives.

The Waste of Worry

Buttons, Lakewood Ranch, FL

Photo by: Aleta Lentz

Worry never robs tomorrow of its sorrow, it only
saps today of its joy.
- Leo F. Buscaglia

I admit it: I'm a recovering worrier. I have a long history of worrying, and I learned from the master. My dad had elevated worrying to an art form. It wasn't until the final months of his life when he truly learned to live in the moment. During my last visit with him, when he was already very ill, he told me how he'd learned to "appreciate every flower, and every butterfly." It sounds trite, but it resonated deeply with me, coming from a man who had spent so much of his life doing the exact opposite.

I was also fortunate that I had a feline master teacher who showed me how useless worrying is. During her illness, Buckley taught me how to stay in the moment and not get ahead of myself with worry. Even on her bad days, she did not waste precious moments worrying about things like a bad test result or a poor prognosis.

And yet, I can't seem to completely break the habit. I suppose it's because I'm not a cat, I'm a human with all the flaws and shortcomings of the species.

Worry is a complete waste of precious time. When Karl Pillemer, the author of **30 Lessons for Living: Tried and True Advice from the Wisest Americans,** interviewed 1200 elders for his Legacy Project, he heard over and over again that the one thing most people regretted was the time they wasted worrying about the future.

Not too long ago, I had a pretty poignant reminder of this, courtesy of Allegra and Ruby. I've been dealing with some ongoing home repair issues that I had been neglecting. I was really worried about the extent and cost of the needed repairs, and had been sticking my head in the sand for a while, but reached a stage where I could no longer ignore the problem. Now mind you, I spent an amazing amount of time worrying about these issues before I even had my trusted handyman look at the problem. I also always worry about Allegra and Ruby anytime a service person comes by the house. They don't like being locked up in a room, and the hammering and drilling that often accompanies repairs frightens them.

Thankfully, my handyman is a cat guy, and while Allegra and Ruby always greet him at the door, once the hammering starts, they disperse to their various hiding places. For Ruby, that's usually under my bed, for Allegra, it's either inside the kitchen cabinet, under the sofa, or behind the shower curtain in the downstairs bathroom. So really, there was no need for me to worry about the two of them – and yet, I did it anyway.

Turns out the needed repairs aren't going to be nearly as daunting as I had feared. We'll start addressing them one item at a time, and everything will be taken care of soon.

But what this brought home to me once again was what a giant waste of time worry is. I'm going to try to remember this experience the next time I get caught up worrying about something. And I'm also going to try some of these:

Create a "worry period." Don't make it longer than 5 or 10 minutes, and try to do it at the same time every day. During that period of time, you can worry about everything and anything you want. Let yourself go crazy. Imagine the worst case scenario. But that's the only time of the day you get to do that. The rest of the day is a worry-free zone. If any thoughts of worry come up during the day, jot them down, then let them go. Remember, you can worry about them during your worry period. Chances are that after a few days of doing this, you'll realize how pointless worrying is, and those 5 to 10 minutes will seem like a ridiculously long amount of time.

Keep things in perspective. How many times do things really turn out as bad as you feared? It's kind of like the man who said: "Don't tell me worrying doesn't work! Almost everything I worry about never happens to me!"

Accept that you're not in control. Thinking about everything that could go wrong doesn't make life any more predictable. Sometimes, things just happen. You may not be able to control the situation, but you CAN control how you react.

Be more like your cats. Cats don't know how to worry. They live in the moment. Something either feels good, or it doesn't. If it doesn't, they'll let you know so you can change it for them. Now who's the smarter species?

![Photo of Nilla the cat]

Cats are Soul Savers

Nilla, Santa Fe, NM

Photo by: Susan Spicer

There is no soul that love cannot save.
– Carlos Santana

There are hundreds of folk tales and superstitions surrounding cats, and one of them is that cats steal a dead person's soul. Of course we know that that's ridiculous. In fact, the opposite is true: cats are good for the soul.

People may fall into one of two categories: soul suckers or soul savers. But there's no doubt in my mind that all cats are soul savers.

You probably know a soul sucker or two. Soul suckers are always negative, angry and judgmental. They get their kicks out of dividing people. They trade their soul for some perceived power over others; a power that exists only in their own minds. They're the ones who always come up with warnings about everything. They leave nasty comments on blogs and on Facebook. Life is always hard, things are always bad, and they just know the world is going to hell in a hand basket. They suck all the energy out of a room, and they want everyone around them to commiserate and live the same miserable lives they do.

Soul savers, on the other hand, see the beauty and light in the world. Just being around them feels good. They believe that basic goodness exists in all of us. They don't deny that there is pain and suffering in the world, but they don't constantly share stories of struggle and misery. They are compassionate, and they care for others and uplift them. They're good listeners. They are there for others when they're needed, but they won't allow others to indulge in self-pity and negativity.

Doesn't that describe purr-fectly what cats do for us?

Cats remind us to live in the moment, to slow down, and not take life so seriously all the time. If that's not the work of a soul saver, I don't know what is.

Transformational Purrs

Are You Too Set In Your Ways?

Anya, Salt Lake City, UT

Photo by: Will Hodges

You will either step forward into growth, or you will
step backward into safety.
– **Abraham Maslow**

One of the reasons I love cats so much is that they're creatures of habit. I love my daily rituals, from that first cup of coffee while I sit on my loveseat and contemplate the world outside my window to tucking myself into bed with my cats at night. But I've come to realize that there's a fine line between enjoying routine, and being set in your ways.

By definition, a routine is something that we do regularly, without thinking much about it. Once established, routines become a consistent part of our lives. Positive routines include meditation, exercise, eating regular healthy meals, spending time with family and friends, and doing things we love. Because routines don't require us to constantly make new decisions, they help us live a more relaxed life. And when we're more relaxed, there's more balance in our lives, and more time to focus on the things that really matter.

The definition of being set in your ways is doing the same thing every day, and not wanting to change those habits, even if they no longer serve you.

So having a routine and liking it isn't necessarily a bad thing, but being so set in your ways that there's no room for change in your life is. Martha Stewart once said, "When you are through changing, you are through." I think she's on to something.

One of the many joys of single life and having no one but Allegra and Ruby to answer to is that I can structure my life anyway I want. For me, that means a mixture of routine, and spontaneity. I try to keep a balance, but lately, the balance has tipped to a little too much routine, so I decided to mix things up a little. Every day, I try to change at least one habit, even just a little.

Here are some suggestions on how to shake up your routines so you don't end up being too set in your ways:

- **Walk a different route.** I have several loops for my daily walks, and most days, I don't really think about which loop to take, I just seem to end up on the same loop each day. Lately, I make a conscious effort to change it up every day. It was quite amazing to me how this seemed to free up mental space and increased my creativity. This also works if you're driving the same route to work each day: change it up once or twice a week.

- **Brush your teeth with the opposite hand.** You'll be surprised how challenging this is!

- **Wear something in a bold new color you normally wouldn't wear.** Lately, I've been finding myself drawn to colors I don't usually like, such as orange or teal.

- **Choose an activity you loved as a child, and try it again.** Making mud pies? Lying on your back watching the clouds? Indulge yourself. You may be surprised at how this changes the way you feel.

- **Order something different at your favorite restaurant.** Even though I eat out a lot, I tend to order the same few dishes at the restaurants I go to the most. By being more adventurous, I've discovered some wonderful new items.

- **If you have a favorite spot where you sit when you read or watch television, change it up and sit somewhere else.** Fair warning: your cats, being the creatures of habit they are, may not appreciate this one. I tried this one evening, and Allegra and Ruby were so confused, they wouldn't settle down until I went back to my usual spot. While I'm all for changing my life for the better, I, of course, would never do it at the expense of my cats' comfort!

When Work Becomes Play

Ruby and Allegra

Photo by: Ingrid King

I don't think of work as work, and play as play.
It's all living.
– Richard Branson

Richard Branson, to me, has always been the epitome of someone who has turned his passions into a successful business. I consider myself extremely fortunate that I get to do what I love for a living, and much of my work feels like play. I love working from home, and being my own boss. But with all this freedom come some challenges when it comes to what is known in popular parlance as "work life balance." I can't remember the last time I worked an eight hour day, and I definitely can't remember the last time when I took an entire weekend off. But does it really matter, when I love my work?

Richard Branson's quote made me realize that it doesn't. Work or play – it really is all living. What does matter is that you do everything with a sense of joy. Robert Frost once said "When work becomes play, and play becomes your work, your life unfolds." This has certainly been true for me – and I consider myself very fortunate that I've been able to build this life for myself.

This does not mean that you should become one-dimensional. As much as I love writing and spending time online connecting with my readers, it can't be all I do. There is more to life than sitting in front of a computer. Ultimately, it is about balance. But perhaps, that balance is easier to achieve when you stop compartmentalizing your life, and instead, work on harmonizing all aspects of your life so that you don't have to think about it in terms of work or play, busy time or down time, time spent online or offline, but rather, you think of all of it as an expression of your soul's desire – and it all becomes living.

There are a lot of different ways to go about living your life with a sense of joy. Richard Branson has written numerous books about how he became successful in business and in life. Your definition of success may not be the same as Mr. Branson's, but his advice applies to more than just building a successful business. If you need a jump start to living a joyful life, consider the following quotes attributed to Mr. Branson:

- ○ I enjoy every single minute of my life.

- ○ The majority of things that one could get stressed about, they're not worth getting stressed about.

- ○ I can honestly say that I have never gone into any business purely to make money. If that is the sole motive, then I believe you are better off doing nothing.

- ○ If you can indulge in your passion, life will be far more interesting than if you're just working.

- ○ I love what I do because every single day I'm learning something new.

If work and play aren't quite the same for you, start small. If you could do anything, what would it be? Take one small step toward it. It may be as simple as connecting with one other person who is already doing what you'd like to be doing, and taking them out to lunch.

![Cat photo]

The Platinum Rule

Silk, Beaverton, OR

Photo by: Peg Silloway

How people treat other people is a direct reflection of
how they feel about themselves.
– **Paulo Coelho**

We've all heard of The Golden Rule: "Do unto others as you would have them do unto you." Many of us strive to live by this rule. It implies the basic assumption that other people would like to be treated in exactly the same way you would like to be treated.

Then there's The Platinum Rule: "Treat others the way they want to be treated."

Think about it for a moment. The Golden Rule is all about you: you simply assume that everyone should want what you want, and you're going to treat them accordingly. This approach is really not so much about others, it's about you. It's all about control. This was brought home to me the other day, when Allegra gave me one of her rare lap times. Allegra is a super sweet, affectionate cat, but she does not like to sit in my lap, nor does she like to be held. As a result, the times when she does make one of her rare lap appearances are extra special. As I found myself thinking once again "I wish she'd do this more often," I realized that there was a big lesson there for me to learn. I can't control how she gives back loving – you can't force a cat to sit in your lap when she doesn't want to be there – but I can appreciate how she expresses her love, on her own terms.

According to The Golden Rule, my loving on her should produce reciprocation – she should love on me, in the way I'd like to be loved on: by sitting in my lap and cuddling with me. But that's just not her personality, and I don't love her any less for it.

The Platinum Rule allows me to honor her for the unique cat she is, and to give her loving in ways that she's comfortable with: by stroking her when she rubs up against me or rolls over on the floor for me, by quietly sitting next to her, by having her tucked against my back when we're sleeping at night.

This, of course, extends to people as well: The Platinum Rule accommodates the feelings of others. The focus shifts from "this is what I would want, so I'm going to give exactly that to the other person" to "let me first understand what they want and then I'll give it to them."

Dale Carnegie once wrote, "You can make more friends in two months by becoming interested in other people than you can in two years by trying to get other people interested in you." He then adds, "When dealing with people, let us remember we are not dealing with creatures of logic. We are dealing with creatures of emotion, creatures bustling with prejudices and motivated by pride and vanity."

Hmm. Was he really talking about cats?

Get Over it

Fifi, Fairfax Station, VA

Photo by: Andrea Tasi

What's broken is broken — and I'd rather remember it
as it was than mend it and see the broken
places as long as I live.
– Margaret Mitchell

Life's disappointments can knock the wind out of the best of us, and sometimes, it seems like we'll never get over some of the bad things that happened to us over the course of our lives. Human tendency can be to continue to bring up the painful past, rather than working on healing the pain and moving on with our lives.

Cats don't do this. They live in the moment. They don't dwell in the past and constantly revisit it, nor do they use the past as an excuse for not being happy in the present. This is particularly evident with cats who were rescued from marginal or abusive circumstances. It is humbling to be loved unconditionally by an animal coming from a rough beginning. While some of these cats may initially be cautious around humans, most of them adjust quickly once they find their forever home and a person who is willing to be patient and allow the bond between cat and human to develop slowly so that it can turn into trust and eventually love. Cats do not allow their early life experiences to define them the way so many humans do.

So why is it so hard for humans to just "get over it?"

Back in 1994, the Eagles released their first single after a 14-year breakup, and it was titled "Get Over It." I always liked the lyrics, delivered with Don Henley's trademark sarcasm:

> You drag it around like a ball and chain
> You wallow in the guilt, you wallow in the pain
> You wave it like a flag, you wear it like a crown
> Got your mind in the gutter, bringin' everybody down
> Complain about the present and blame it on the past
> I'd like to find your inner child and kick its little ass
> Get over it
> Get over it
> All this bitchin' and moanin' and pitchin' a fit
> Get over it, get over it

This concept was brought home to me even more dramatically the other day when I was doing Reiki on Fifi, a 17-year-old cat in renal failure. Fifi is my veterinarian's cat. Dr. Tasi shared some of her background with me: Fifi was 7 years old when she was brought to the veterinary clinic where Dr. Tasi worked at the time. She had a spinal tumor, and her hind legs were paralyzed. Her owner never returned for Fifi, and Dr. Tasi ended up adopting her. Fifi went through several rounds of chemotherapy, and regained function in her legs again. She adjusted beautifully to Dr. Tasi's multicat household.

One day, Dr. Tasi decided to consult with an animal communicator for all her cats. As one of her other cats shared his story of a rough background (all of her cats are rescues), Fifi interrupted. The animal communicator relayed that what she was "saying" was clearly "We all have our stories – just get over it!"

Fifi may be on to something. While there is certainly value in looking back and understanding how our past impacts our present in terms of preferences, behavior, and emotional challenges, there is a tipping point where prolonged analysis of past wrongs can result in bringing more of the same into our lives. By living in the moment, appreciating the gifts we have in our lives, and letting go of the past, we free ourselves for a better and happier tomorrow. Each moment offers us a choice—to look back at what did not work for us in the past or to look forward and invite the chance for a new beginning and for change toward a happier life.

I think we might do well to take Fifi's advice.

Is Your Cat a Mirror of Yourself?

Ruby

Photo by: Ingrid King

Life is a mirror and will reflect back to the thinker
what he thinks into it.
– Ernest Holmes

One of the most fascinating concepts in the area of personal growth to me has always been the concept that every single person in your life is your mirror. Others reflect back aspects of our own consciousness to us, giving us an opportunity to see ourselves in a different light, and ultimately, to grow. Sometimes, that reflection may come from someone we greatly admire. Other times, it may come from someone who aggravates us and pushes all our buttons. It's the latter reflection that may lead to exponential personal growth, if we allow ourselves to explore the concept.

It struck me the other day that if this applies to the people in our lives, could it also apply to the cats in our lives? Do our cats reflect back aspects of ourselves? Is this, perhaps, especially true if we live with a "less than purr-fect" member of the feline species, such as a cat who exhibits behavior problems, or simply doesn't quite act the way we'd like her to?

I started to look at Allegra and Ruby: what aspects of their personalities do I share? Of course, being human, I looked for positive aspects first. Both Allegra and Ruby like their routines – and so do I. They are sun worshippers – and so am I. They like having their meals served to them – I hate to cook, and love to eat out.

While both of my girls are little angels most of the time, there are some aspects of their personality that can be a little challenging. Was it possible that those sides of their personalities were reflected in me?

Allegra is quick to react when something annoys or startles her. I have a tendency to jump to judgment too quickly. Ruby sometimes makes bad decisions: batting at Allegra while she's settling down on one of our window perches for a nice long nap is a surefire way of getting herself hissed at and bopped on the head. I've been known to make decisions too hastily, not always considering all possible outcomes, and then regretting that I didn't take more time.

I found the exercise fascinating, especially from the perspective of looking at personality traits that may no longer serve me, such as the quick jump to judgment. I'm a firm believer that cats come into our lives to teach us to stretch and grow. Maybe this mirroring is just another way they help us live fuller and more conscious lives.

Meditate With Your Cat

Tiger, Foster City, CA
Photo by: Stella Chen

Where there is peace and meditation, there is
neither anxiety nor doubt.
– St. Francis de Sales

The benefits of meditation are endless: from helping us handle stress better to getting in touch with our true spiritual nature, meditation has been proven to make our lives better. In fact, there is so much evidence that meditation is good for you that it seems like meditation should be as much a part of our daily lives as breathing.

Once you've established a daily meditation practice, you can't imagine not having it in your life, but until you get there, the thought of daily mediation seems to bring out a long list of excuses for most people: "I don't have the time," "I don't know how," "I can't sit still."

You don't have to meditate for hours to gain benefits from meditation. Even a 5 minute mini-meditation can make a difference. Gradually increase the time. Ideally you want to meditate at least 20 minutes a day.

And if you need more inspiration to get started, look to your cats! Cats are natural meditators. What else do you think they're doing when they're sitting with their paws curled under, their gazes soft, and not a care in the world? Of course they're meditating!

And because they're such little Zen masters, they can help us get comfortable with meditation. If you feel resistance to getting started with a meditation practice, try meditating with your cat.

How to meditate with your cat:

1. Sit with your cat while she's relaxed. She can be next to you, in your lap, or simply in the same room. Make sure you sit in a comfortable position. If sitting cross-legged on the floor or a cushion is comfortable for you, that's ideal, but sitting in a chair is fine, too. Try to keep your spine fairly erect.

2. Relax your eyes and soften your gaze. You can look at your cat, or you can look at a spot in front of you. You can also close your eyes. Do what feels comfortable.

3. Focus on your breath. Don't exaggerate your breathing, just breathe in and out naturally, and observe how the breath feels.

4. If you find yourself getting distracted by thoughts, simply bring your attention back to your breath. Don't chastise yourself for thinking – silently say to yourself "thinking," and return to focus on your breath. Be gentle with yourself – you're not a failure at meditation just because you can't empty your mind.

As you relax deeper into this meditation, you'll start feeling a sense of peace. Your connection with your cat may feel even deeper than it normally does. And in the process, you will reap all of the benefits of meditation. Now why wouldn't you want to make this a regular practice in your life? I'm sure your cat would want you to!

![cat sitting in window perch looking outside]

Take Time for Yourself

Frank, Chichester, NH

Photo by: Barbara Crawford

Sometimes the most important thing in a whole day is
the rest we take between two deep breaths.
– Etty Hillesum

We all have busy lives, and there are days when it feels like we'll never get everything done. For most people, the first thing to fall by the wayside during busy times is taking time for yourself. I've never met a cat who has said, "I'm too busy to take a moment to stretch in the sun." Why can't we be more cat-like when it comes to taking care of ourselves?

The following ten tips can help you carve out some time for yourself even when the world is screaming for your attention. I offer this thought to you: you can't afford not to take the time. Your sanity, and your health, may depend on it.

1. Say no to anything that's not important. I've always liked Stephen Covey's system of sorting items on your to-do list into urgent, important, not urgent, and not important categories. Surprisingly, it's the items in the "important but not urgent" quadrant, not the things that are "urgent and important," that should receive your greatest attention. For example, daily playtime with your cats is important but not urgent. Feeding your cats, however, is important and urgent! For a more detailed (and less cat-centric) explanation of Covey's important/urgent matrix, read Covey's **7 Habits of Highly Effective People**.

2. Ask for help. Frequently, people who are constantly busy are actually admired by others, because they appear to be so efficient and get so much done. Our society does seem to value busyness, and some people even consider it a badge of honor – a very warped view, in my opinion. Admit that you can't do it all by yourself. You may be surprised at the response you get. Most people love to help others.

3. Meditate. Even a five minute mini-meditation at the beginning of your day can set the tone for a less stressful day. Better yet, take a few mini-meditation breaks during the day.

4. Write things down. When you're busy, your mind is usually working overtime. Writing things down anchors them somewhere other than in your mind, which will help you remain calmer.

5. Set limits for yourself and stick with them. Allot times to specific tasks, and stop after your allotted time is up. There are so many things in life that will never be completely "done." Celebrate your progress, and don't beat yourself up over what isn't finished yet.

6. Reward yourself. Give yourself small rewards for tasks you've accomplished. Whether it's a piece of chocolate (just don't go overboard with this, and go for the good stuff), or a walk around the block, even small rewards can serve as small motivators.

7. Unplug. Cut back on your online activities. Turn off your cell phone, even just for a few hours.

8. Make time for exercise. Even though exercise probably seems like just one more item on your overflowing to-do list, this is one activity you want to make a priority.

9. Breathe! Take deep, cleansing breaths whenever you feel yourself getting overwhelmed.

10. Spend time with your cats, and learn from them. Just being in their presence will remind you that the things that really matter in life are right there in front of you, curled up on that cozy pillow, or sleeping in that sun puddle on the floor.

Why Crossing Your Challenge Line is Good for You

Calypso, Eagan, MN

Photo by: Pat Wolesky

Life's challenges are not supposed to paralyze you,
they're supposed to help you discover who you are.
— **Bernice Johnson Reagon**

Cats are creatures of habit. This may be one of the thousands of reasons why I love these gorgeous creatures so much: I love my routines, and change doesn't always come easily for me, despite the fact that most, if not all, change in my life has always been for the better. And there's nothing wrong with positive routines. When the Dalai Lama was asked "if you only had one word to describe the secret of happiness, and of living a fulfilling and meaningful life, what would that word be," he replied without hesitating: "routines."

But there is a lot to be said for moving outside of your comfort zone. In fact, stepping out of your comfort zone may be crucial to your personal growth, creativity and success.

Jackson Galaxy coined the term "challenge line" in his work with cats. The challenge line is the point where a cat crosses from comfort ("I think I'll just stay under the bed, it's safe down here.") to challenge ("Let's see. I may be shy, but maybe there's more fun to be had in the rest of the house?"). Jackson uses the challenge line to push cats just past their comfort level to see how they react, because, he says, "then I know exactly what I can do to benefit the cat."

It's up to us as cat guardians to help our cats cross that challenge line, but when it comes to our own lives, we carry the sole responsibility for pushing ourselves outside of our comfort zone. Trying new things and stretching may be uncomfortable at first, but ultimately, it will help us grow.

Increase your creativity. Stepping out of your comfort zone makes you more creative. Sharing creative work carries an innate risk: you're opening yourself up to rejection and criticism. The most successful people fail more often than those who never take risks.

Become more adaptable. Challenging yourself past your comfort zone makes you more adaptable to change in general. Once you've experienced that you can step out of your comfort zone and succeed, unexpected changes won't feel like such a daunting experience.

Age more gracefully. For many people, their comfort zone gets smaller as they get older – yet another reason to push past it more frequently. By forcing yourself to move past your challenge line and embracing new experiences, you remain fully engaged in life, and as a result, your life will become richer.

Stepping across your challenge line doesn't need to happen in big leaps. Start by taking small steps. Sometimes, something as simple as taking a different route to work can shift your perspective.

Philosophical Purrs

Random Acts of Kindness

Sir Mojo and General Jaxson, Rockledge, FL

Photo by: Holly England

My religion is very simple. My religion is kindness.
– The Dalai Lama

Have you ever been the recipient of a random act of kindness? Maybe someone let you go ahead in the grocery store line because you only had one item. The driver in the car ahead of you at the toll booth paid your toll. A friend you haven't talked to in a while called for no reason at all. If you've been on the receiving end of such an act of kindness, you know how wonderful it feels.

Research suggests that positive emotions help contribute to better physical and emotional health. Small random acts of kindness can brighten anyone's day – and the nice thing is, they make both the giver and the recipient feel good. Here are some suggestions:

- Hold the door open for someone.

- Give up your seat on the subway.

- Smile at someone, just because.

- Leave a larger than normal tip.

- Look a homeless person in the eye when you offer them food or money.

- Send a greeting card to a friend for no reason at all.

Do cats perform random acts of kindness? Sometimes, I think they do. Allegra is not much of a lap cat, but there are times when, out of the blue, she'll jump up on my lap and settle in for a short nap. Unlike Ruby, my little Velcro cat who is in my lap all the time, these moments are so random, and special, that they could quite possibly be Allegra's way of a random act of kindness toward me.

Cats Create Human Connections

Django, Ashburn, VA

Photo by: Renee Austin

Whether we like it or not, there is hardly a moment of our lives when we do
not benefit from others' activities. For this reason it is hardly surprising that
most of our happiness arises in the context of our relationships with others.
– Tenzin Gyatso, 14th Dalai Lama

We all long for genuine connection with other human beings. Connecting with others not only makes life richer, it appears that we are actually wired to form relationships with others. In **Social: Why Our Brains Are Wired to Connect**, psychologist Matthew Lieberman explores groundbreaking research in social neuroscience, revealing that our need to connect with other people is even more fundamental than our need for food or shelter.

Genuine connection feeds the soul. Connection feeds the soul. We need it to be happy, it expands our lives, boosts creativity, and opens our world to opportunities we might otherwise not even be aware of. In this world of social media, it has never been easier, or harder, to connect with others. Easier, because there's always someone online that you can "talk" to, and harder, because genuine connection requires more than just an occasional "like" or comment while scrolling through your Facebook newsfeed.

Cat connections. For me, a lot of the connections in my life have been brought about by cats. Fifteen years ago, after my first soul mate cat Feebee had passed away, I went to a local pet loss support group. This was long before there was Facebook, and online communities were in their infancy. The leader of the group became one of my closest friends. I firmly believe that Feebee had a paw in sending me to that first meeting.

He also led me to my career in veterinary medicine, which ultimately, although in a bit of a roundabout way, led to my writing career. And once I started writing, the floodgates opened: Buckley, through her book, Amber, through the website she inspired, and now Allegra and Ruby, have connected me with thousands of cat lovers around the world.

Are online connections genuine connections? A recent survey by Petsmart Charities of 1,023 people found that more than half of the cat guardians surveyed said they talk about their cat or share cat videos online. The internet has become the cat guardian's version of the dog park.

Are all of these connections genuine? I think they are. The community on our Facebook page is more than 174,000 strong. The Conscious Cat reaches about 150,000 readers each month. Do I have a connection with each and every one of these followers? Not in the traditional sense. But I do feel that we're all part of the same community, united by our common love for cats and the desire to make their lives as good as they can be.

Many of my "cat-induced" connections began as online friendships, but have become treasured "real life" friendships as time went on.

Connections help us grow. Since most of life's most profound lessons happen as a result of our interactions with others, perhaps, cats also facilitate connection so that we may grow beyond what we might even imagine to be possible.

I feel blessed to have all of these cat connections in my life. In this day and age, nobody needs to ever be really alone, except by choice. Connection is only an email, a blog post, a phone call, or a get-together away. And for me and many others, it's all because of these amazing and beautiful and special cats.

Accepting What Is

Abby, Decatur, AL
Photo by: Toni Nicholson

Happiness can only exist in acceptance.
– **George Orwell**

Every single moment in life offers us a choice: we can either be in the moment and accept what is happening, or we can resist it. This is a lesson that life tends to present to us over and over. Whether it's weather throwing a wrench into our plans, or a friend or co-worker not cooperating with our wishes, gracefully accepting what is can be challenging.

Resistance is part of human nature. We want things to be a certain way, and when they're not, we start complaining. Weather is a prime example. Grumbling about the weather is often a favorite pastime, and I'm frequently guilty of participating in these types of conversations. However, after a few times of thinking or saying "I'm so sick of this weather," I usually realize just how much of an energy drain it is to resist something you can't control.

Acceptance is a choice. While we can't always control what is happening in our lives or in the world around us, we can choose how we react. We can choose to accept what is happening or we can struggle against it. Accepting what is will result in a peaceful state of mind, while struggle will only lead to misery.

Acceptance does not mean that we agree with what is happening, and it does not preclude change. In fact, acceptance is usually the first step toward lasting change.

A positive mindset. Life doesn't always give us what we want, no matter how positive we think, but a positive mindset will help us embrace what is happening. Acceptance is the springboard to dealing with challenges in a more productive, and ultimately more peaceful way. I believe that every challenge comes with a lesson, and finding the reason behind why something is happening can make a big difference in how you deal with it.

Acceptance is not an easy practice, but it is a rewarding one. Cats seem to be good at it. Perhaps it's because they have mastered living in the moment, and acceptance is about mindfulness and being present.

Accepting what is. It turned out that once I made the decision to stop complaining about the weather, I found myself appreciating each day and each season for its unique gifts. I found myself slowing down in general rather than trying to rush through life, trusting that things will unfold in their own time.

And I look to Allegra and Ruby for clues. Even though they may complain about the lack of sun puddles on a cool, cloudy day, they quickly find another comfy spot to nap in rather than being unhappy.

Taxes, Gratitude and Cats

Tuxie, Leonardstown, MD

Photo by: Laurie Van Gorden

The hardest thing in the world to
understand is the income tax.
– Albert Einstein

I think it's safe to say that the chore of working on the annual tax return is everyone's least favorite task. Of course, depending on your record keeping system, tax preparation can be a delight for your feline assistants. After all, what's more fun than diving into a shoebox full of receipts and watching them fly all over the place?

I spoil the fun for Allegra and Ruby by not using a shoebox system. My bookkeeping software, along with a pretty well organized file system, makes tax time about as painless as it can get, but every year, there's still that moment, when I see my CPA's number on the caller id, when I have to take a deep breath and brace myself for the bottom line. I have been blessed with a steadily growing business, which, of course, means that every year, I pay a little bit more in taxes.

People usually complain about having to write a check to the IRS, about how much they have to pay in taxes, and about how everything just keeps getting more and more expensive. This seems to be the prevailing "story" and it makes for good conversation around the water cooler and in social situations, because it's something everybody can agree on, right?

I've been guilty of participating in those types of conversations, but I really try to avoid that line of thinking, because it is based in lack. I'm not suggesting that simply thinking about having money is going to create money, but I do think it's beneficial to change how you think and talk about taxes, and about money in general. Thoughts and words carry energy, and that energy impacts how you live your life, as well as the choices you make – choices that extend beyond just financial decisions.

I've been trying to change my story and think about money from a place of gratitude, rather than lack. Rather than being angry at the IRS for "taking my hard earned money," I'm grateful that I have a successful business. Rather than resenting writing that check to the electric company, I'm grateful that they've kept me warm all winter long. I know it's a leap in consciousness, but shifting how you view money can make a big difference.

Ultimately, gratitude is about living in the present moment – something our cats excel at. The energy of gratitude is a powerful force. It can shift your mood and your thoughts from a place of scarcity to a place of abundance and joy.

The Gift of Jealousy

Polar Bear, Magnolia, TX

Photo by: Bari Dubois

To cure jealousy is to see it for what it is: a
dissatisfaction with self.
– Joan Didion

Jealousy is a complex emotion that everyone experiences at one time or another. It's human nature to compare ourselves to others. And yes, cats get jealous, too.

Jealousy can be toxic. It makes you feel small and petty. On the face of it, jealousy seems to be directed at the other person, but ultimately, the only one suffering is you. It's not easy to admit to being jealous, because it means facing your own insecurities and fears. Jealousy feels awful, and allowing yourself to indulge in it will almost always damage your soul.

But there's a gift hidden inside the jealousy you feel. Uncovering that gift can be hard work, but if you allow yourself to confront the green-eyed monster, you will be surprised at the insights you'll gain into your own psyche.

Jealousy is a reflection of something inside yourself. Instead of being jealous of someone else, look inward. Why are you reacting so strongly to someone's good fortune? When you feel jealous, it's always about wanting what they have. If you really want it, what's stopping you from getting it? Are there real obstacles to getting what you want, or are you letting your fears and insecurities hold you back?

Jealousy forces you to be honest with yourself. When you're jealous of someone's achievements, or of something they have, ask yourself why you want what they have. Why does their success bother you so much? What is at the root of your jealousy? Do you really want your sister's boyfriend, or is it a sense of connection that you're looking for? Do you really want your friend's work schedule, or are you looking for more freedom? Try to identify the essence of what it is about a person or situation that is making you jealous. You may be surprised at what comes up for you.

Jealousy can be a catalyst for change. Chances are that the person you're jealous of doesn't have the perfect life you think they have. But the fact that you're jealous is a clear indication that you're unhappy with something in your own life. Use your jealousy to figure out what you want to change in your life, and let it fuel your journey.

Jealousy between cats. Cats do experience jealousy, and it is rooted in the same reasons as human jealousy: insecurity, and a perception that there's not enough. Jealousy among cats is usually the result of a new cat or baby coming into the family. The cat feels that the change affects her normal life and the amount of attention she receives. Jealousy can lead cats to react with aggression, or by retreating and hiding. The key to dealing with a jealous cat is to reassure her that there's enough love to go around for everyone. This means introducing any change, especially a new family member, gradually, and sharing the gift of your love and attention equally.

Ruby occasionally gets a little jealous of Allegra. Ruby is my little lovebug. She's happiest when she's in my arms or on my lap. If she had her way, she'd probably be permanently glued to me. Allegra is a little more reserved with showing her affection, but lately, she has been giving me a little more lap time. Ruby is not sure how she feels about that, but we're working through it.

Cats as a Pathway to Spiritual Connection

Pearl, Middleburg, VA

Photo by: Nancy McMahon

When people go within and connect with themselves,
they realize they are connected to the universe and
they are connected to all living things.
– Armand Dimele

Connecting with our spiritual core is an important part of conscious living. We all have different ways of doing this, and there isn't any one single method that is more valuable than another. For some, it may be through structured religious observations, often shared in the community of a church or other spiritual gathering. For others, this connection may happen during meditation. Others still may connect with spirit in nature. Watching a beautiful sunset or sunrise, walking in a deep green forest, or hiking in a striking desert landscape – all of these can help open a portal for a connection to something greater than ourselves.

Whether we call this something God, our soul, Spirit, or Source, I believe that all humans have an innate need to feel this kind of connection. We know it when we have it. Sometimes, it may just be for a brief, almost fleeting moment. Other times, we may be able to bask in it for an extended period of time. Regardless of how it comes about and how long it lasts, the feeling that comes with it is one of utter peace, joy, and love. It's that feeling we get when we're completely absorbed in doing something we love. We lose track of all sense of time. We are living in the present moment, to the exclusion of everything else. Anything is possible, and magic can and will happen.

Animals, especially cats, have always helped me find that spiritual connection. Animals are so much closer to nature than we are, and as such, are much more in touch with Spirit than most humans. Simply observing a cat can instantly transport me into a state of connection.

In **Zooburbia: Meditations on the Wild Animals Among Us**, Tai Moses writes, "We can trust animals to be themselves, and because of that, in some ineffable way, they help connect us to a better part of ourselves, to the more authentic self we long to be. In their inability to be anything but genuine, animals remind us of the ways in which we are imperfect and the ways in which we can be a little kinder, a little more generous, a little braver."

I believe that animals facilitate this connection with our true self. That moment, when we simply observe a sleeping cat, or play with her, or pet her, forces us to step back from our busy lives for a little while, and to just be in the moment. It's during those moments that we are reminded of who we really are, and that we're connected to something greater than ourselves.

Acknowledgments

Being a writer is a solitary profession, but no book is created by the writer alone. This was never truer than for the creation of this one. My deepest appreciation goes out to all of you who submitted photos of your beautiful cats. I wish I could have included all of them.

I would also like to express my profound gratitude to the following:

To my Conscious Cat readers, for being a part of our community, and for reading and sharing what I write every day. I am honored and humbled that my writing is making a difference in so many lives, both feline and human.

To everyone at Mango Media, for your enthusiasm about this book, and for making it a reality.

To my inner circle – you know who you are. I wouldn't be who I am without your friendship, encouragement and unwavering belief in me.

And last, but not least, to my feline teachers: Allegra, Ruby, Amber, Buckley, and Feebee. Thank you for the love, purrs, and inspiration.

About the Author

Ingrid King is the award-winning author of **Buckley's Story: Lessons from a Feline Master Teacher, Purrs of Wisdom: Conscious Living, Feline Style,** and **Adventures in Veterinary Medicine: What Working in Veterinary Hospitals Taught Me About Life, Love and Myself.** She is a former veterinary hospital manager. Her popular blog, The Conscious Cat, is a comprehensive resource for conscious living, health, and happiness for cats and their humans. The Conscious Cat has won multiple awards, including DogTime Media's Pettie for Best Pet Blog in 2011, 2012, 2013, and 2014, and About.com's 2012 Readers Choice Award for Best Website About Cats. Ingrid lives in Northern Virginia with her tortoiseshell cats Allegra and Ruby. For more information about Ingrid, please visit **www.ConsciousCat.com.**

Ingrid King with Ruby

Do you have questions or comments?

I'd love to hear your thoughts. Email me at **consciouscat@cox.net**.

If you're not already a reader of The Conscious Cat, I'd love to invite you to join one of the best communities of cat lovers on the Internet. **www.Consciouscat.com**

One last thing

If you have enjoyed this book, I would love it if you would take a few moments to post a review on Amazon or share it with your cat-loving friends on Facebook and Twitter.

CPSIA information can be obtained
at www.ICGtesting.com
Printed in the USA
BVOW11s0808220316
441275BV00001B/1/P

9 781633 532892